MW00685973

Pomegranate

SAN FRANCISCO

Paintings
NEW OF
YORK

MUSEUM OF THE
CITY OF NEW YORK

A BOOK OF POSTCARDS

Pomegranate Communications, Inc.
Box 808022, Petaluma CA 94975
800 227 1428; www.pomegranate.com

Pomegranate Europe Ltd.
Unit 1, Heathcote Business Centre, Hurlbutt Road
Warwick, Warwickshire CV34 6TD, UK
[+44] 0 1926 430111; sales@pomeurope.co.uk

ISBN 978-0-7649-5780-2
Pomegranate Catalog No. AA662

Pomegranate publishes books of postcards on a wide range of subjects.
Please contact the publisher for more information.

Cover designed by Gina Bostian
Printed in Korea
20 19 18 17 16 15 14 13 12 11   10 9 8 7 6 5 4 3 2 1

To facilitate detachment of the postcards from this book, fold each card along its perforation line before tearing.

come thirty paintings made between 1825 and 1993. They capture many aspects of New York, from the unveiling of the Statue of Liberty to a night scene of a street in the Bowery. The artists range from gifted amateurs to professional artists who specialized in marine subjects, a muralist, and the celebrated American impressionist Childe Hassam.

A city perpetually in motion, New York changed most visibly between 1857, when the design competition for Central Park was won by Frederick Law Olmsted and Calvert Vaux, and 1931, when the Empire State Building established supremacy over the Manhattan skyline. The expansion of green, the surge of skyscrapers, and the vault of suspension bridges attracted countless artists to set up their easels, chronicling the changing metropolis. They recorded feats of engineering and new leisure areas, the parks and squares where New Yorkers strolled and sauntered.

During the same period, the population of New York shot from two million to seven million, stuffing the land so tightly that subsequent increases have been relatively modest. Artists could hardly ignore the change, and their pictures captured the press of throngs at parades and waterfront entertainments.

The great poet of America's greatest city, Walt Whitman asked in "Sun-Down Poem" (later retitled "Crossing Brooklyn Ferry") "Ah, what can ever be more stately and admirable to me than mast-hemm'd Manhattan? / River and sunset and scallop-edg'd waves of flood-tide?" How much more might he have admired the island a century after his song, when towers stood like masts all across the land!

Paintings OF NEW YORK

George Loring Brown (1814–1889)
View of Central Park, 1862
Oil on canvas, 20 x 42 in.
Museum of the City of New York
Gift of Miss Lillian Draper, 72.42

707 782 9000   WWW.POMEGRANATE.COM

Pomegranate

Paintings OF **NEW YORK**

Joseph Oppenheimer (1876–1966)
Madison Square, 1900
Oil on canvas, 30 x 34 in.
Museum of the City of New York
Gift of the artist, 50.165
Courtesy of the Joseph and Fanny Oppenheimer Foundation

707 782 9000   WWW.POMEGRANATE.COM

Pomegranate

Paintings OF NEW YORK

John M. Slaney (active 1890s)
Gapstow Bridge, 1895
Watercolor on paper, 7¾ x 9½ in.
Museum of the City of New York
The J. Clarence Davies Collection, 89.4.1

WWW.POMEGRANATE.COM

707 782 9000

Pomegranate

NEW YORK CONNECTING RAILROAD BRIDGE AT HELL GATE

Paintings OF **NEW YORK**

James Monroe Hewlett (1868–1941)
New York Connecting Railroad Bridge at Hell Gate, c. 1916–1917
Oil on canvas, 35 x 60¼ in.
Museum of the City of New York
Gift of Mr. Lloyd Hornbostel and Mr. Caleb Hornbostel in memory
of Mr. Henry Hornbostel, 62.117.1

707 782 9000   WWW.POMEGRANATE.COM

Pomegranate

Rockefeller Center — David Litwin ~ 1941

Paintings OF NEW YORK

Israel C. Litwak (1867–1952)
Rockefeller Center, 1941
Oil on canvas, 26½ x 40¼ in.
Museum of the City of New York
Gift of Mr. and Mrs. Leo Treem, 86.56
© Estate of Israel Litwak

707 782 9000   WWW.POMEGRANATE.COM

Pomegranate

Paintings OF **NEW YORK**

Ruth Carroll (1899–1999)
Elevated Station, c. 1929–1930
Oil on canvas, 25 x 30¼ in.
Museum of the City of New York
Gift of the artist, 80.163.1

707 782 9000   WWW.POMEGRANATE.COM

Pomegranate

Paintings OF **NEW YORK**

Everett Warner (1877–1963)
The Municipal Building, c. 1915
Oil on canvas, 50 x 40 in.
Museum of the City of New York
Gift of the artist, 41.182.1
Courtesy Thomas E. Warner, Archivist for the
Everett Warner Archives

707 782 9000   WWW.POMEGRANATE.COM

Pomegranate

Paintings OF **NEW YORK**

Sebastian Cruset (1859–1943)
View from Queensboro Bridge During Snowstorm
on St. Patrick's Day, 1910
Oil on canvas, 14⅛ x 28⅛ in.
Museum of the City of New York
Gift of Fong Chow in memory of his grandfather,
Sir Shouson Chow, 73.228

Pomegranate

707 782 9000   WWW.POMEGRANATE.COM

Paintings OF **NEW YORK**

W. S. Parkes
Crystal Palace, c. 1853
Oil on glass backed with mother-of-pearl, 34 x 46 in.
Museum of the City of New York
Gift of Mrs. Samuel S. Schwartz, 64.94

707 782 9000   WWW.POMEGRANATE.COM

Pomegranate

Paintings OF **NEW YORK**

George Harvey (1801–1878)
Nightfall, St. Thomas Church, Broadway, New York, c. 1837
Watercolor on paper, 8⁵⁄₁₆ × 13⅝ in.
Museum of the City of New York
Bequest of Mrs. J. Insley Blair in memory of
Mr. and Mrs. J. Insley Blair, 52.100.11

707 782 9000   WWW.POMEGRANATE.COM

Pomegranate

Paintings OF **NEW YORK**

Warren Sheppard (1858–1937)
Brooklyn Bridge Celebration, May 1883, 1883
Oil on canvas, 24 x 40 in.
Museum of the City of New York
Lent by Edward C. Gude, L779

707 782 9000   WWW.POMEGRANATE.COM

Pomegranate

Paintings OF NEW YORK

Fred Pansing (1844–1912)
Sampson and Schley Leading the Fleet into New York Harbor,
August 20, 1898, c. 1898
Oil on canvas, 19 x 42 in. (framed)
Museum of the City of New York
Gift of Dwight Franklin, M31.94.7

707 782 9000   WWW.POMEGRANATE.COM

Pomegranate

Paintings OF NEW YORK

Stokely Webster (b. 1912)
Times Square, 1940
Oil on canvas, 24 × 20 in.
Museum of the City of New York
Gift of the artist, 75.40

707 782 9000 WWW.POMEGRANATE.COM

Pomegranate

Paintings OF **NEW YORK**

Maurice Kish (b. 1898)
East River Waterfront, 1932
Oil on canvas, 44 x 36 in.
Museum of the City of New York
Gift of the artist, 72.41

707 782 9000   WWW.POMEGRANATE.COM

Pomegranate

Paintings OF **NEW YORK**

Frederick Detwiller (1882–1953)
Temples of God and Gold, c. 1923
Oil on canvas, 52¾ x 44 in.
Museum of the City of New York
The Robert R. Preato Collection, 91.76.17

707 782 9000   WWW.POMEGRANATE.COM

Pomegranate

BLENDON·REED·CAMPBELL·

Paintings OF **NEW YORK**

Blendon Reed Campbell (1872–1969)
The Queensboro Bridge, c. 1935
Oil on canvas, 40 x 54 in.
Museum of the City of New York
Gift of Mrs. Alice C. Flenner, 71.121

707 782 9000   WWW.POMEGRANATE.COM

Pomegranate

Paintings OF **NEW YORK**

Bascove (b. 1946)
Pershing Square Bridge, 1993
Oil on canvas, 26 × 42 in.
Museum of the City of New York
Museum purchase, 94.81
© Bascove

707 782 9000   WWW.POMEGRANATE.COM

Pomegranate

Paintings OF **NEW YORK**

Childe Hassam (1859–1935)
Winter Afternoon in New York, 1900
Oil on canvas, 23 x 19 in.
Museum of the City of New York
Bequest of Mrs. Giles Whiting, 71.120.107

707 782 9000   WWW.POMEGRANATE.COM

Pomegranate

Paintings OF NEW YORK

John Beverley Robinson (1791–1863)
Jefferson Market Court House, 1881
Watercolor on paper, 16⅛ x 14¾ in.
Museum of the City of New York
Gift of the Estate of Beverley and Winnafred Robinson, 82.27

707 782 9000   WWW.POMEGRANATE.COM

Pomegranate

Paintings OF **NEW YORK**

Ernest Fiene (1894–1965)
Night View, St. Patrick's Cathedral, 1956
Oil on canvas, 35⅞ x 24⅛ in.
Museum of the City of New York
The Robert R. Preato Collection, 91.76.4
© and courtesy Estate of Ernest Fiene

707 782 9000   WWW.POMEGRANATE.COM

Pomegranate

Paintings OF **NEW YORK**

Benjamin Eggleston (1867–1937)
Brooklyn Bridge, c. 1927–1930
Oil on canvas, 48⅛ x 38 in.
Museum of the City of New York
The Robert R. Preato Collection, 91.76.7

707 782 9000   WWW.POMEGRANATE.COM

Pomegranate

Paintings of **NEW YORK**

Anthony Imbert (1794–1834)
The Erie Canal Celebration, New York, 1825, 1825–1826
Oil on canvas, 24 x 45 in.
Museum of the City of New York
Anonymous gift, 49.415.1

707 782 9000   WWW.POMEGRANATE.COM

Pomegranate

Paintings OF **NEW YORK**

James Cafferty (1819–1869) and Charles G. Rosenberg (1818–1879)
Wall Street, Half Past Two O'clock, October 13, 1857, 1858
Oil on canvas, 50 x 40 in.
Museum of the City of New York
Gift of the Honorable Irwin Untermyer, 40.54

707 782 9000   WWW.POMEGRANATE.COM

Pomegranate

Paintings OF **NEW YORK**

William Louis Sonntag Jr. (1869–1898)
Madison Square Garden, c. 1895
Watercolor on paper, 22½ x 15 in.
Museum of the City of New York
Gift of Mrs. Frederick A. Moore, 49.14

707 782 9000 WWW.POMEGRANATE.COM

Pomegranate

Paintings OF NEW YORK

Childe Hassam (1859–1935)
Rainy Late Afternoon, Union Square, 1890
Oil on canvas, 35½ x 43½ in.
Museum of the City of New York
Courtesy of Miss Mary Whitney Bangs, 69.121.1

707 782 9000   WWW.POMEGRANATE.COM

Pomegranate

Paintings OF **NEW YORK**

Leo McKay (dates unknown)
Steeplechase Park, c. 1898–1906
Oil on canvas, 51 x 80 in.
Museum of the City of New York
Gift of Mrs. George C. Tilyou, 54.167

707 782 9000   WWW.POMEGRANATE.COM

Pomegranate

Paintings OF **NEW YORK**

William Louis Sonntag Jr. (1869–1898)
The Bowery at Night, c. 1895
Watercolor on paper, 13 x 17¾ in.
Museum of the City of New York
Gift of Mrs. William B. Miles, 32.275.2

707 782 9000   WWW.POMEGRANATE.COM

Pomegranate

Paintings OF **NEW YORK**

Grace Ravlin (1873–1956)
Red Cross Parade, Fifth Avenue, at 41st Street, 1918
Oil on canvas, 25¼ x 30 in.
Museum of the City of New York
Gift of the Women's Association of the Brick Presbyterian
Church, 56.90

707 782 9000   WWW.POMEGRANATE.COM

Pomegranate